KOSHAL STATE WHY ?

JAYA PRAKASH PRADHAN

KDF Working Paper No. 1, 2004

Koshala Development Forum

New Delhi-110 067

The Koshala Development Forum (KDF) is an informal research forum constituted by the students of JNU belonging to the Koshala region of Orissa (Anugul, Bargarh, Bolangir, Boudh, Debagarh, Jharsuguda, Kalahandi, Kandhamal, Koraput, Malkangiri, Nabarangapur, Nuapada, Rayagada, Sambalpur, Sonepur, and Sundargarh district) with the support from the students of other parts of India for creating awareness about the problem of underdevelopment and deprivation in the Koshala Region. The region, which is infamous for illiteracy, poverty, starvation, and child-selling, has been the most neglected part of modern India and since Independence it has seen the rarest forms of deprivation. In this context, the struggle of Koshali people for the creation of an independent state is significant for decentralization process in India, as well as for ensuring that development percolates to the neglected region. The Forum, being apolitical, non-violent, and democratic, is meant to promote the general understanding on the problems of development of the Koshala region through discussions, public meetings, seminars and research publications.

Contents

Acknowledgements

We thank Selvam V. for going through the draft and giving his useful comments. Encouragements received from all KDF members and supporters are also gratefully acknowledged.

1

I
Introduction

The demand for 'Koshala State' in Orissa has recently become intense following the creation of three new Indian states namely Chhatisgarh, Uttaranchal and Jharkhand. The news headlines frequently captured the growing popular support for Koshala movement in Orissa. 'A new state out of Orissa in 5 years?'[1]; 'Sambalpur Municipality adopts resolution for Koshala state'[2]; 'Ferment in Orissa'[3], 'Demand for Koshala state gains momentum in Orissa'[4]; 'Stir for 'Koshala State' to be intensified'[5]; 'MLA seeks statehood for western Orissa'[6]; 'Demand for separate Koshala state gets boost in western Orissa'[7]; 'Pro-Koshala campaigners gear up to intensify stir'[8]; and 'Cry for Koshala'[9] are few of the headlines to mention. This popular sentiment in Koshala for a separate state is in complete contrast to the Koshali people's leading role in the establishment of Orissa as a separate state way back in 1936.

[1] Indiainfo.com (2000) 'A new state out of Orissa in 5 years?', available at http://newsarchives.indiainfo.com/2000/10/06/kosala6.html

[2] Orissa.net (2000) 'Sambalpur Municipality adopts resolution for Koshala state', February 11.

[3] Frontline (2001) 'Ferment in Orissa: Even as the movement seeking statehood for western Orissa gains momentum, the State government renews its demand for special category status for Orissa', Vol.18, Issue 15, Jul. 21 - Aug. 03.

[4] Daily Excelsior (2003) 'Demand for Koshala state gains momentum in Orissa', June 01.

[5] Hindu (2003) 'Stir for 'Koshala State' to be intensified', October 20.

[6] Hindustan Times (2003) 'MLA seeks statehood for western Orissa', October 14.

[7] Hindustan Times (2003) 'Demand for separate Koshala state gets boost in western Orissa' November 17.

[8] Pragativadi (2003) 'Pro-Koshala campaigners gear up to intensify stir', December 13.

[9] Deccan Herald (2004) 'Cry for Koshala', January 04.

Under the British rule the Koshala region loosely called Sambalpur region, which was under the Chhota Nagpur Division of the Central Provinces, had seen replacement of Oriya by Hindi as the official language in 1895 (Sahu et. al. 2001). This has led to long drawn popular movements in the region for the cause of Oriya language and culture. The Koshali people led by Nilamoni Vidyaratna, Dharanidhar Mishra, Madan Mohan Mishra, Braja Mohan Patnaik, Balabhadra Supakar, Bihari Das and others had spearheaded the movement for restoration of the Oriya as the official language and transfer of the Sambalpur region including Patna, Kalahandi, Sonepur, Bamara and Rairakhol to the Orissa Division of the Bengal Province. The vernacular press, Sambalpur Hitaisini, published from Bamra has played an important role in sustaining and encouraging the movement. As a result of prolonged struggle by the Koshali people supported by the Coastal people, on 16 October 1905 Sambalpur region was amalgamated with the Orissa division. This was the first historical step in the struggle of the Oriya people for the formation of a separate Orissa Province later in 1936. As the Oriya language consists of Koshali dialect (loosely called Sambalpuri) and Coastal dialect, the creation of Orissa province has seen greatest sacrifice made by the Koshali people to accept coastal dialect as the official language even though Koshali remain as the sole language of their daily existence. Many Koshali people like Gangadhar Meher, Bhima Bhoi had contributed significantly towards Oriya literature based on the coastal dialect.

The Koshali people had not only played a pivotal role in constructing the modern identity of Orissa state but also had made significant contribution towards the development and progress of the state. The Koshali population, according to Census 2001, account for about 39 percent of the Orissa population[10] and the Koshala region make-up about 59 percent of the total area of the Orissa state[11] (see Appendix-A for Map of proposed Koshala state). They contribute nearly 45 percent of total workers and 48 percent of total cultivators in Orissa[12]. The Koshala region is the source of about 76

[10] Koshala region comprising of 16 districts namely, Anugul, Bargarh, Bolangir, Boudh, Debagarh, Jharsuguda, Kalahandi, Kandhamal, Koraput, Malkangiri, Nabarangapur, Nuapada, Rayagada, Sambalpur, Sonepur, Sundargarh have a population of 143 lakh as compared to total Orissa population of 367 lakh.

[11] The total area of Koshala region is about 92, 200 sq. kms. as compared to 155, 707 sq. kms. of total area of Orissa (source: Authors based on Orissa Economic Survey 2002-2003, pp. ANX-26)..

[12] According to 2001 Census, the total workers and cultivators in Koshala region are estimated to be 64 lakh and 20 lakh respectively. Orissa is estimated to have 143 lakh of total workers and 42 lakh of cultivators.

percent of net value-added generated in the Orissa manufacturing[13]. In terms of forest resources, it contributes the highest percentage of forestland in Orissa with 66 percent of the total Orissa forest area[14]. Further, Koshala is the richest source of minerals comprising iron ore, manganese ore, base metals (copper ore and lead ore), bauxite, china clay, coal, fire clay, graphite, limestone, dolomite, and precious minerals including diamond[15] in Orissa. In fact the share of Koshala in the total reserve of minerals is 99 percent in the case of bauxite; 100 percent each in the case of coal, dolomite, lead & zinc, and limestone; 30 percent in iron ore; and 28 percent in the case of manganese ore[16]. Its share in the value of mineral exploited in Orissa ranges from 100 percent in the case of Coal as well bauxite to 27 percent in the case of iron ore to 22 percent in the case of manganese ore during 2001-2002[17]. In the case of Orissa's own tax revenue, Koshala contribute about 39 percent of total sales tax and excise duties each, 33 percent of entertainment tax and motor vehicle tax each, 32 percent of general cess and nistar cess, and 30 percent of land revenue[18].

[13] In 1996-97 the net value-added in Orissa is Rs.222434.2 lakh of which about Rs. 168,952 lakh originate in the Koshala region (Source: Authors

based on http://ori.nic.in).

[14] The forest-covered land of the Koshala region is 38,129 sq. km. in 2001-02. That of Orissa is 58135 sq. km. for the same year (Source: Authors based on Orissa Economic Survey 2002-2003, Annexure Table-6.1, pp. ANX-26).

[15] The iron ore deposits occur in the Bonai-Keonjhar belt of Sundergarh district, Gandhamardan, and Hirapur of Nowrangpur district; the manganese ore occurs in Koraput, Kalahandi, Bolangir, and Kandhamal districts; the base metal ore occurs in the old Sambalpur district; bauxite occurs in old Koraput, Kalahandi, Bolangir and Sambalpur districts; coal deposits occur in Anugul and Sambalpur districts; fire clay occurs in Anugul, Jharsuguda and Sundergarh districts; graphite deposits occur in Bargarh, Bolangir, Kalahandi, Kandhamal, Rayagada, and Anugul districts; limestone and dolomite deposits occur in Sundergarh, Bargarh, Koraput and Malkangiri districts; and precious minerals including gem stones occus in Sambalpur, Anugul, Deogarh, Jharsuguda, Bolangir, Sonepur, Kalahandi, Nawapada and Rayagada districts (see Sinha (1999) pp. 224-251 for more details).

[16] In 1999-2000, Orissa has been estimated to have a total reserve of 1730.18 million tonnes of bauxite (of which 1720.18 million tones occurs in Koshala region), 43.54 million tones of coal (which completely occurs in Koshala region), 433.05 million tones of dolomite (which completely occurs in Koshala region),

2.51 million tones of lead & zinc (which completely occurs in Koshala region), 1032.18 million tones of limestone (which completely occurs in Koshala region), 3555.33 million tones of iron ore (of which 1051.05 million tones occurs in Koshala region), and 49.01 million tones of manganese ore (of which

13.96 million tones occurs in Koshala region). (Source: Authors' calculation based on http://ori.nic.in/diorissa/tb53.htm).

[17] Source: Authors' calculation based on Orissa Economic Survey 2002-2003, Table-10.6, pp. 10/6.

[18] The data which relate to the year 1989-90 has been obtained from Statistical Abstract, Orissa, 1991, Table-21.06, pp. 228-230. It should be noted that the presented figures on the share of Koshala region in tax revenue are an underestimation as the data on Angul district is not available separately and hence could not be included in the Koshala region. Angul is an important district of Koshala which has estimated to have contributed

about Rs. 405 crore revenue to the Orissa state's coffers in 2002-03, of which coal royalty was Rs. 217.86 crore, sales tax was Rs 102.92 crore, goods and passenger tax was Rs. 31.91 crore, motor-

It is against this backdrop that the paper intends to investigate the factors responsible for Koshali people's demand for a separate state when they themselves were the main propagator for a unified Orissa state in the past. Majority of the coastal Orissa people treats this demand to bi-furcated Orissa as politically motivated without really understanding the problems of the Koshala region. They fail to appreciate the fact that the demand for Koshala state lies in the real issues of livings that the Koshali people have faced rather than in the political motivations[19] and hence it essential that the debate over Koshala state in Orissa should be based on proper perspectives rather than unquestioned sermon of one-state-identity.

The paper has been organized as follows. Section 2 examines several factors responsible for the demand of the Koshala state in Orissa. Sub-section 2.1 analyzes the role of hunger and poverty in explaining the rise of the demand for Koshala state in Orissa. Sub-section 2.2 examines the large-scale distress out-migration from Koshala region and the Orissa government's lack of concern in addressing the issue. Sub-section

2.3 discusses the continuing educational deprivations at primary, secondary and tertiary levels faced by the Koshala region. Sub-section 2.4 examines the health security of the Koshali population and critically evaluates the role of the state in the provision of the same. Sub-section 2.5 looks into the regional disparity that characterizes the Koshala region relative to the Coastal region of Orissa in terms of access to basic infrastructure such as access to transport, communication, banking, energy, and irrigation. Sub-section

2.6 evaluates marginalization of Koshali culture, language and literature by the state as another important factor lending to the support for a separate state. Sub-section 2.7 explores the state apathy in developing tourism sector of Koshala region. Section 3 concludes the paper.

II

Factors Behind the Demand for Koshala State

The demand for Koshala state can be seen as a part of the growing popular movements in India for the creation of smaller states such as movements for Telangana in

vehicle tax was Rs. 10.69 crore, and taxation on electricity was Rs. 21.70 crore (Source: Orissa.net (2003) 'Angul contributes Rs 405 crore to State coffers', April 16).

[19] Political motivation may be one reason for this demand but it is not among the most important factors which range from economic to cultural factors as discussed later in the paper.

Andhra Pradesh, Vidarbha in Maharashtra, Harit Pradesh in Uttar Pradesh, Gorkhaland in West Bengal, and Bodoland in Assam. The demand for creation of smaller states in a country with relatively greater degree of heterogeneity of the population in terms of tastes, preferences and income over space and other geographical diversity like climate has the backing of compelling advantages of spatial and fiscal decentralization which would results in improved resource allocation in the public sector. Smaller states ensure that the decision-making process involves greater participation of the people, civil society and delivers flexible, immediate and effective actions under greater accountability and good governance. They are more efficient in providing public services and infrastructure evenly over locations, as their size is small and thus have low levels of regional disparity in terms of development as compared to larger states. Their greater ability to establish partnerships with private sectors, mobilize local skills, develop local transport, health, energy, and so on could be significant for overall growth and development of a particular country.

However, the demand for smaller states including Koshala state in India have risen not on the grounds of the perceived economic benefits of smaller size but mostly because of the prolonged underdevelopment and backwardness that these regions have faced. In the case of Orissa the process of economic growth has been regionally lopsided during the last fifty-years. While the coastal region has benefited mostly from the economic policies pursued by the sate, the Koshala region remains largely neglected, marginalized, and deprived. The regional imbalances has been such an extent that the news of starvation death, child-selling for rice, large-scale illiteracy, malnutrition, distressed out-migration etc. have came to be the characteristics of Koshala region. The feelings of Koshali people that they remain neglected even though they had contributed a lot in constructing modern Orissa state has been the single most important factor in voicing their demand for an independent state of Koshala. The fact that the Koshala region contributes significant chunk of resources for the Orissa government in the form of sales and excise tax, land revenues, mining, kendu leafs, timber, bamboo, fire wood and other forest products but get least attention in the public expenditure to address the basic necessities of human development such as education, health, access to safe drinking water, roads, etc. has embolden the recent struggle for Koshala state.

III

Poverty

The incidence of chronic poverty in Koshala coupled with government failures in addressing its rising trends has been the most important factor for the demand for a separate state in Orissa. Majority of Koshali people lacked minimum purchasing power to meet even square meals per day let alone the minimum purchasing power required for buying food to fulfill the nutritive requirements of a healthy human being embodied in the official construction of poverty line. In the infamous backward districts of Koshala region of the KBK (Koraput, Bolangir and Kalahandi) about 68.8% persons live below the poverty line and even the Chief Minister of Orissa recognized the region to be the poorest region in India[20]. Recurrent droughts, inadequate irrigation, skewed land distribution, stringent forest laws denying forest right to the villagers[21], and a rigged market and state laws that promote exploitative monopolies in the grain and forest product markets[22]all together have made Koshala a 'hunger belt' in Orissa over the half- century since Independence. The results have been a human-disaster including large-scale starvation deaths, child selling, out-migration and malnourishments serialized by various Indian as well as international newspapers.

The highly under-estimated government figures on hunger deaths in Orissa indicate that out of 441 deaths reported in the state during 2000 to 2003, 268 deaths alone were from Koshala region . With 72 starvation deaths Rayagada stood as the highest starvation-prone Koshali district followed by Kalahandi (34), Koraput (32), and Bolangir (27). The real figure on starvation deaths in the Koshala region is surely more than what is reported as the state government headquartered in the Coastal region usually tends to dismiss any starvation death in Koshala region as baseless. But

[20] See the address speech of Shri Naveen Patnaik, Chief Minister, Orissa, to the 49th National Development Council (N.D.C.) Meeting on 1st September 2001, Vigyan Bhavan, New Delhi.

[21] InterPress Service (1999) 'India: Loss of Forest Control Impoverishes Orissa Villagers', November 23.

[22] Asia Times (1999) 'Hunger, disease stalked Orissa long before cyclone', November 17.

due to tremendous pressures from media, judiciary[23], National Human Rights Commission (NHRC)[24], and opposition protests in the state assembly[25] the Orissa government has finally released these under-estimated figures on starvation deaths. In the famous Kashipur starvation deaths incident in the Koshali district of Rayagada the district collector has summarily rejected any starvation deaths in the district and attributed the cause of deaths to the food habits of the local people eating mango kernel resulting in food poisoning[26].

Apart from manifesting in starvation deaths the acute level of poverty in Koshala region shows its ugly face in the form of child-selling. Although the news of child-selling dates back to 1985 when Phanas Punji, a thirty year old woman shocked the nation by selling her fourteen year old sister-in-law Banita Punji to one Vidya Podh for Rs 40 to

[23] Orissa.net (1998) 'Starvation deaths alleged in Balangir dist HC seeks Govt report in 15 days', November 21

[24] Orissa.net (2002) 'NHRC pulls up State Government for starvation deaths', November 22.

[25] Orissa.net (2000) 'Hunger deaths trigger angry protests', December 08; Orissa.net (2000) 'Govt grilled over continuing hunger deaths', December 15.

[26] Hindu (2001) 'Orissa deaths: Abject poverty comes into focus', August 31.

buy food for her children in the Koshali district of Bolangir. Since then the number of child selling in the Koshala region has risen dramatically[27]. The government of Orissa has recognized that during 2000-2003, 14 babies were sold by their parents at a price rate ranging between Rs.10 to Rs.200 in the Bolangir district alone[28]. The latest in this series has been the case of Sumitra Behera of Anugul district selling her newborn baby to Gayash Behera for only Rs. 10 due to starvation[29].

The severity of poverty in the Koshala region can be guessed from the fact that on an average, monthly per capita expenditure of every 45 out of 100 Koshali households falls below a minimal amount of Rs. 300 and 36 households lie in the range of Rs.300 to Rs. 500 per capita, these two together stands to be 81 household . As compared to only 25 out of 100 households in the Coastal region falls in the per capita monthly expenditure of Rs. 300 category, nearly half the number of household observed in the case of Koshala region. Similarly, the Koshala has the largest concentration of low- income household in Orissa even while considering the case of rural areas. Taking the monthly per capita expenditure as surrogate measure of poverty simply suggests that the Koshala has a higher percentage of population living below the poverty line as compared to the Coastal region in Orissa. The Engel's ratio which is the proportion of food expenditure to total consumption expenditure is invariably lower in the case of Coastal region as compared to Koshala region further indicating that the standard of living is lowest in Koshala region.

The district-level poverty statistics of Orissa suggest that about 69 percent of Koshali household live below the poverty line in 1999-2000 . This is about 14 percentage points higher than the poverty figure of the Coastal region in Orissa. It is most important to note that between 1987-88 and 1999-2000 the percent of household below the poverty line has gone up in the case of Koshala region whereas it has come down in the case of Coastal region. The fact that the poverty ratio for three undivided Koshali district such as Kalahandi, Koraput and Phulbani were even higher than 80 percent indicates the abject nature of poverty in the Koshala region. The modest decline in the poverty ratio was during 1987-88 to 1993-94 but it had been a reversal trend during 1993-94 to 1999-2000.

The apathy of Orissa government to the incidence of poverty in Koshala region has been most unfortunate in the last half a century. Whenever any news on starvation deaths appears in newspaper the first official reaction of the state government has been to simply deny such incident. The non-seriousness in the government response to the issue of poverty and starvation death in the Koshala region had manifested in several cases of

improper implementation of the projects sponsored by the central government meant for backward districts of Koshala region as noted by the planning commission of India [30].

Over the years the government policy document has been added with ever increasing number of new welfare schemes worth several hundreds of crores of rupees from the central and state government but the economic conditions of the poor remain unchanged in the Koshala region. The success of welfare measures such as the Integrated Rural Development Programme (IRDP), Development of Women and Children in Rural Areas (DWCRA), Training of Rural Youth for Self Employment (TRYSEM), Supply of Improved Toolkits to Rural Artisans (SITRA), Ganga Kalyan Yojana (GKY), Million Wells Scheme (MWS), Employment Assurance Scheme (EAS), the Swarnjayanti Gram Swarozgar Yojana (SGSY) and most recently the Sampurna Gramina Rozgar Yojana (SGRY) (integration of JGSY and EAS) can be judged from the fact that poverty is increasing in the Koshala region in the 1990s.

The benefits from anti-poverty schemes hardly reached to the actual poor in the majority of the cases as official poverty line do not include them[31]. Take the case of Kashipur block of Rayagada district where only about 15 percent of the population has been provided the BPL card though the people of the locality are known to be very poor and whoever have got in majority of cases have mortgaged their BPL cards to local moneylenders and liquor traders[32]. The BPL list prepared by the state government which includes the Orissa energy minister A.U. Singhdeo, who is the scion of the Bolangir royal family; his nephew, K V Singhdeo, who is the industry minister; and the latter's wife and BJP MP from Bolangir Sangita Singhdeo[33], indicates the fact that how the actual poor families of the rural Koshala region are benefiting from the welfare schemes being implemented. Various poverty alleviation programmes in Orissa have failed due to rampant corruption, unawareness of schemes amongst beneficiaries and wrong targeting of the beneficiaries[34]. In many cases, the poor people of the Koshala region even cannot

[30] Utkal Sambad (2004) 'Improper Utilization of funds in KBK districts: Planning Commission expresses concern', March 4.

[31] Orissa.net (2001) 'It's official – 95 pc live below poverty line', September 28; Orissa.net (2001) 'Thanks to Govt , they happily stay below poverty line', January 25.

[32] Hindu (2001) 'Orissa deaths: Abject poverty comes into focus', August 31. [33] Times of India (2002) 'Even the royals are now poor in Orissa', January 07. [34] Orissa.net (2002) 'Anti-poverty schemes a farce in Orissa', December 10.

buy subsidized rice supplied through the public distribution system (PDS) due to lack of purchasing power.

Further, the minimal developmental resources meant for Koshala region including poverty alleviation schemes has been systematically siphoned-off from the region to the coastal region through corruption. The government officials in Koshala region including block development officer (BDO), junior engineer, gram panchayat extension officer, village level workers (VLWs) and other officials who happen to be mostly from Coastal region of the state and who strive to avoid being posted in the region. They take least interest in any development work at local level and get satisfied with their commissions[35]. The News Channel, NDTV, reported the acknowledgement of a government official about the system of paying commissions to a whole lot of people including senior officials and politicians even from the funds meant for Food for Work schemes undertaken by the government of Orissa in the drought-affected districts of Koshala region[36]. The large-scale misappropriation of Central aid coming under various social security schemes can be seen from the famous September 22, 1999 report of the then deputy administrator (Hrushikesh Panda) of the KBK (undivided districts of Kalahandi, Bolangir, Koraput) that had elaborated upon the widespread misappropriation of funds given by the Centre under agreement with the International Fund for Agriculture Development (IFAD) and the role of the then district collector, two directors of the IFAD project, and many other government officials forcing Central government to withhold the aid to the poverty-ridden Kashipur block of Rayagada [37]. The Hrushikesh Panda report noted that not a single plant claimed to have been planted under the programme can be traced, payments were made against non-existent works, roads were built from no where to no where, estimates of works were recklessly revised and only non-tribals were handpicked as contractors by the officials[38].

[35] Dreze (2001) based on the candid admission of one contractor in Bhawanipatna provide the following account of the commissions that were "due" to various officials for any development work at the panchayat level: 3 per cent for the BDO, 5 per cent for the junior engineer, 5 per cent for the "gram panchayat extension officer", 5 per cent for the block chairman, 2 per cent for the block clerk, 2 per cent for the block cashier.

[36] NDTV (2001) 'Misuse of funds discovered in Orissa's Food for Work scheme', June 12.

[37] Times of India (2001) 'In Orissa, funds for the poor are siphoned by babus', September 01; Times of India (2001) 'Centre withholds Rs 130 cr aid for Kashipur', September 05; Times of India (2001) 'Orissa govt takes action against three officials', September 04.

[38] Times of India (2001) 'In Orissa, funds for the poor are siphoned by babus'

The corruption money going into the account of bureaucrats straightly shifted to the Coastal region as majority of them belongs to that region. The commissions going to local politicians also get transferred to the Coastal region as their actual habitation lies in the state capital Bhubaneswar rather than in the name-sake rural buildings kept in the Koshala region for election purposes.

This failure of the state government in checking corruption and properly addressing the grinding poverty in the Koshala region and the corrupted role played by government officials who invariably belong to the Coastal region has naturally fueled discontentment among general Koshali people that they have not received their right share of development even though they are contributing major chunk of resources towards the state. The present Prime Minister of India, Shri Atal Bihari Vajpayee summed up the developmental disparity in Orissa as follows:

"After touring western Orissa and interacting with the people of the region, I have come to the firm conclusion that the development of this part of the State, although rich in natural resources like mineral deposits and forests, has been neglected. This has resulted in the impoverishment of the people of this region, which has been left way behind by the developed areas of the State... The stark reality of poverty, hunger, starvation, illiteracy and malnutrition that one witnesses in vast tracts of western Orissa is further highlighted by the fact that

the bulk of the people who have been denied a share of the development cake are tribals... In a sense, western Orissa is the real face of India. It is a matter of shame that fifty years after Independence people should die of hunger; that parents should be forced to sell their children for a fistful of rice". [39]

IV

Distress Out-Migration

The decades of chronic poverty, recurring droughts, unemployment, backwardness and developmental exclusion by the state have led to the emergence of the Koshala region as a source of large-scale distress out-migration in Orissa[40]. The available figures indicate that from the two Koshali districts namely Bolangir and Nuapada alone an estimated 200,000 labourers migrate annually[41]. Traditionally a larger chunk of

[39] The statement issued by Shri Atal Bihari Vajpayee on Koshala (Western Orissa) is available at http://www.bjp.org/BJP Statements -Statement issued by Shri Atal Bihari Vajpayee.htm

[40] Hindu (2004) 'Searching for jobs, they leave their votes behind', April 03.

[41] Asia Times (1999) 'Hunger, disease stalked Orissa long before cyclone', November 17.

migration from the Koshala region used to be during the non-agricultural season but years of recurrent drought and unavailability of employment is now forcing tens of thousands of Koshali people to migrate from the region throughout the year. Increasing level of migration also happening in the Coastal region of Orissa but the nature of migrant differs from that of the Koshala region. The migrants from the Coastal region are in general economically better-off and educated and they migrate to other states mainly in search of better employment opportunities, and not so much because of desperate search of livelihood in the face of drought or famine, like people in the Koshala region[42]. The migrants from Koshala region are starkly poor and illiterate, migrate to work as casual labourers in the unorganized sectors such as construction sites, brick kilns, pull rickshaws, textiles, etc. in Chhattishgarh, Andhra Pradesh, Gujarat, Maharashtra and West Bengal.

In the absence of regulations and improper enforcement of labour laws these illiterate migrant workers are exploited in various ways. They are compelled to work for long hours at measly wages in the workplace, which is devoid of basic amenities and health security. Take the case of nearly 30,000 migrant workers from Koshala working mostly in brick kilns in and around Hyderabad. Reportedly majority of these workers came here through contractors who trap them with a minimum advance of Rs 5,000 to Rs 8,000 for a group of three persons (Chowdhury 2004). After a long hours of hard work from dawn to dusk and sometimes beyond, this labour force could make 1,000-1,200 bricks which fetch them just around Rs 60 to Rs 110 per day depending on the quality of the bricks. This labour force gets a weekly payment of Rs 300 to Rs 400 from the owner and rest of their salary goes into the repayment of the advance. Their work contract is like bonded labour, never allowing them to even take a day off.

Their living conditions are characterized by lack of basic sanitations, subsistence budget which in turn forcing them to consume substandard food to save up enough money to return home leaving them malnourished, their children remain deprived from schooling and amusements. As labour migration through contractors remains illegal and unaccounted activity, there is no way to ensure compensation in the case of accident, sickness, disability or death of a migrant worker. Recently there has been a phenomenal

[42] Narasimham (2004) 'Money talks...and walks', *Humanscape*, Vol. XI, Issue III, March.

increase in the number of women including pregnant one joining the flow of seasonal labour migration from the Koshala region raising further issues of gender discrimination in wages, women facing increased health risks and threats of sexual exploitation[43]. Several newspapers are reporting cases of sexual abuse of female workers and selling of child labour from Koshala region in other parts of India[44].

The government of Orissa is well aware about this large-scale distress migration from Koshala region and the problems faced by these migrant workers. However, till date this issue has not been looked into by the state to devise mechanism to check distress migration and ensure that whoever is migrating should get right work and proper living conditions. The continuing indifference of the state government to address the plight of lakhs of uprooted poverty-stricken people due to recurrent droughts in the Koshala region has been a significant factor shaping the demand for Koshala state. The Koshala Sangharsha Vahini (KSV) which is leading the movement for a separate state listed the distress migration of Koshali people to other states to work as bonded labour as ninth factor in its list of factor for 'Why Koshala?'[45]. The Koshali migrants have realized that the Coastal-dominated state government is completely insensitive to their issues and failed to address the real issues faced by them[46]. The Koshali people are increasingly viewing recurrent droughts as a result of decades of discrimination unleashed against the region and reckless destruction of natural resources in the region like, forest, and rivers by the state government. This factor has led the Koshali people to believe that they have to have their own Koshala state if they need a state government, which is sensitive to their survival issues.

[43] Indian Express (2001) 'Danger -- drought ahead', February 17; Asia Times (1999) 'Hunger, disease stalked Orissa long before cyclone', November 17.

[44] E.g. Times of India (2003) 'Three Dalit minors rescued from rape, bondage', August 28; Orissa.net (1998) 'Child labour sold in Mumbai for four thousand rupees from Kondhamal district', October 16.

[45] See the un-dated pamphlet 'Dear Koshala-loving friends, mothers and sisters, why Koshala state?' of the Koshala Sangharsha Vahini.

46 Yahoo.com (2004) 'Migrant labourers in drought-hit Orissa to boycott polls', March 24, available at

http://in.news.yahoo.com/040324/139/2c6ou.html.

V

Educational Deprivation

Educationally Koshala represents the most backward region in Orissa. In 2001, only about 54 per cent of the Koshali population, aged 7 years and above, was literate whereas this proportion was 70 percent in the case of non-Koshali region termed here as the Coastal region . This means that for every 100 persons there are only 54 persons who can both read and write without reference to any formal education in Koshala whereas there are 70 persons in the case of Coastal region. The gap between literacy rate of Coastal and Koshala further widen in the case of female and rural literacy. Koshala's literacy rates for both male and female remains far behind than what they enjoy in the Coastal region. The deviation of the literacy rates of Koshali districts from the average literacy level of Coastal region reveals that educational deprivation is very significant for many Koshali districts of the un-divided Koraput, Kalahandi, Boudh- Phulbani, and Bolangir areas . For example Malkangiri have a literacy rate of 31 percent which is nearly half the literacy rate of Coastal region. There is only one Koshali district namely Jharsuguda which has got literacy rate marginally higher than the literacy rate of Coastal region and rest of the Koshali districts falls behind relative to the Coastal region.

Koshala has not only lagged behind Coastal in terms of literacy rate but also in terms of formal educational levels. The rate of educational attainment for primary & middle class is the proportion of population with primary & middle class education out of 9-14 aged population. That for secondary & higher secondary and graduation & above it is the proportion out of 15-19 and 20-24 aged population respectively. It can be seen that in all the three levels of education the Coastal region demonstrate superior performance than the Koshala region. The attainment gap has been observed to be highest in the case of primary & middle school level, followed by secondary & higher and graduation & above. Over gender Koshali girls face more deprivation than Koshali boys in the case of first level of education as the attainment gap of female is greater than male but in other two stages of education Koshali male face relatively more deprivation.

The poor performance of the Koshala region as compared to the Coastal region in the primary as well as higher stages of education may have resulted from various factors but the most important may have been the relatively low levels of government educational expenditure devoted towards the region as compared to the Coastal region. It is well recognized that in an underdeveloped and pre-dominantly agrarian economy like Orissan economy, the household investment in education will be lesser due to low levels of returns to education, lack of information as well as lack of educational institutions. For these economies government investment in the form of new schools, strengthening school-related infrastructure such as blackboard, library, etc., and appointing adequate number of trained teachers plays an important role in increasing accessibility of household to the education. Government expenditure in the form of literacy campaigns helps the household in better assessing the returns of investment in education relative to the returns obtained by sending children to work at very early age. Various incentives offered by the government like providing free text books, stationary, uniform, and providing regular cooked meals are also likely to reduce the cost of sending children to schools by the households.

Physical Access to Educational Institutions

Let us now examine the physical access of households to educational institutions in Orissa. With 22791 primary schools the Coastal region has a per school coverage of 104. This indicates that in terms of per school coverage Koshala region has relatively better access to education at primary level of education than Coastal region. The higher per capita coverage of the Costal region is reflective of the higher population density of the region as compared to Koshala region[47]. Therefore, other factors like poverty other than the un-availability of primary schools relative to the Coastal region may have been responsible for the superior performance achieved by the Coastal region in the primary stage of education. It is well documented that thousands of school-going children from Koshala region are forced by poverty to choose work to earn a square meal for their families rather than go to school even if there is availability of schools in the locality[48]. The dropout rate in schools has been reportedly increased to around 50 percent in rural Koshala regions such as in Bargarh on account of poverty driven by frequent droughts[49]. The physical access to education also includes spatial coverage of school availability. In this case Koshali districts such as Koraput, Malkangiri, Nowrangpur, Rayagada, Bolangir, and Kalahandi represents the most deprived districts in that about 12,609 habitations in this part of Orissa are not served by primary schools within a distance of 1 km, and another 10,177 habitations are not served by upper primary schools within 3 km[50].

As far as upper primary, high school and college level performance is concerned the Koshala has relatively higher population coverage than the Coastal region implying that relative scarcity of educational institution may partly explain the lower performance of the Koshala relative to the Coastal in these levels of education.

[47] In 2001 the Coastal region has a population density of 415 nearly two and half times that of Koshala region (159).

[48] Indian Express (1998) 'Forced to choose: Stomach or slate', November 16.

[49] Indian Express (2000) 'Drought spells disaster for the little women of Orissa', December 8.

[50] Hindustan Times (2004) '32 lakh students dropping out of Orissa schools every year', February 4.

From the point of view of the access to university education through availability of educational institutions there has been a very strong sense of educational deprivation in the Koshala region of Orissa. It has only one university, namely Sambalpur University, situated at Burla, Sambalpur district catering to the educational needs of 14.3 million Koshali people spread across a geographical area of 98, 034 square kilometers . The Coastal region, on the other hand, host to a total of seven universities with per university catering of 3.2 million Coastal people spreading over a geographical area of 63,507 square kilometers. In terms of number of sanctioned seats at post graduate level (MA/MSc etc. and MPhil) there is glaring regional disparity in Orissa. The two major university of Coastal Orissa together have 2081 seat strength with a seat-population ratio of 93 seats per million population whereas the sole Koshali university, Sambalpur University, has only 723 seat strength with a seat-population ratio of 51 seats per million

population . Inclusion of other five universities to the list of Coastal region will further increase its seat-population ratio relative to that of Koshala region.

Coastal

Utkal University (Bhubaneswar), Berhampur University (Ganjam), North Orissa University (Mayurbhanj), Fakir Mohan University (Baripada), Sri Jagannath Sanskrit University (Puri), Orissa University of Agriculture and Technology (Bhubaneswar) and Utkal University of Culture

The Koshala region also has relatively less number of technical and professional institutions in relation to its population size than the Coastal region. One engineering college in Koshala covered about 24 lakh population whereas it covered merely 9 lakh population in the case of Coastal region . The regional ratio of population coverage in the case of polytechnics is 16: 14 lakh, industrial training institute is 4: 3 lakh, medical college is 143: 12 lakh, homeopathic college is 48: 28 lakh, MCA is 1: 0.2 lakh, and management institution is 36: 9 lakh. This suggests that Coastal population is relatively better endowed with all these instructions as compared to Koshali population. Only in the case of Ayurvedic college Koshala has lower population coverage than Costal region. All the institutions taken together Koshala has one institution to serve 1 lakh population whereas Coastal to serve 0.2 lakh. Therefore, Koshali people have relatively less access to technical and professional institutions in Orissa than Coastal people. Moreover Koshala goes without specialized research institutions as Central Rice Research Institute (Cuttack), Institute Of Physics (Bhubaneswar), Homoeopathic Research Institute (Puri), Regional Leprosy Training & Research Institute (Ganjam), Nabakrushna Chaudhury Development Studies (Bhubaneswar) etc. are located in Coastal region.

Quality of School Education Provided

Apart from the provision of physical access to educational institutions the overall educational development of a region crucially depends upon the quality of education provided. The quality of education is determined by two set of parameters namely efficiency of the teachers and better school infrastructure. Considering the efficiency aspect of the educational services, Koshala has seen relatively low level of quality of education even though it has the backlog of lowest literacy rate in Orissa as compared to Coastal region. Koshala has largest percentage of single teacher schools at primary, primary & upper primary, and primary & upper primary & secondary/ higher secondary levels of school education as compared to Coastal region. Given the wide gender disparity exists in education the presence of female teacher schools can be taken as an indicator of efficiency as it is helpful in encouraging female education as well as in better understanding and solving various problems faced by girl students. In this case also Koshala with highest percentage of no female teacher schools is lagging behind Coastal region at all the levels of school education. Likewise Koshala has the lowest percentage of female teacher in total teacher regionally in Orissa.

The estimated pupil-teacher ratio (PTR) is on the lower side for Koshala as compared to Coastal region which may lead one to the conclusion that the efficiency of education services is relatively higher in the case of former. However, this conclusion is most likely to be wrong in the case of Koshala. The estimated pupil-teacher ratio takes

into account the number of sanctioned teacher post not the actual number of teachers teaching in a school. Since, in the case of Koshala where significant proportion of the teacher post are lying vacant due to non-recruitment by the government, it does not make sense to use the number of teacher on the basis of sanctioned post to estimate pupil- teacher ratio (PTR). Although the exact proportion of vacant post is not available for primary school, one estimate put it at 50 percent of posts in the higher education department in lead colleges at Sundergarh, Bolangir and Kalahandi of the Koshala pocket of the state[51]. Therefore taking account of these vacant posts will inflate the estimated PTR significantly. It would have been better to use average hours of teaching given to the student for PTR but data on it is not available. The figure on PTR may also be misleading as the number of teacher in the tribal dominated Koshala region also includes para- teachers like Siksha Karmi who are less qualified, un-trained and underpaid teachers required to teach in the far-flung rural schools. Another indicator of efficiency is the different level of educational qualification attained by teachers is also found to be on the lower side in Koshala than Coastal region suggesting that teachers in the Koshala region are relatively less qualified.

In terms of the provision of school infrastructure over region mixed picture emerges. As far as the percentage of student enrolled in schools without building and without blackboard is concerned Koshala appears to be lagging behind Coastal but when considering student-class-room ratio (SRC) is concerned it is relatively better-off. The relatively higher SRC in the case of Coastal region can be due to its higher density of population rather than disparity in the school infrastructure per se.

The above discussion suggests that Koshala, which has lowest rate of literacy in Orissa suffers from inadequate institutions at higher levels of education including technical and other professional courses. The quality of school education is relatively at lower level than Coastal region. The fact that Orissa government is not serious in addressing the educational problems in Koshala has been an important contributory factor
in the demand for a new state. The pitiable situation of higher education in Koshala, has been depicted by an Oriya News Paper based in Coastal Orissa, Dharitri, as follows:

"Due to the step-motherly attitude of the state government, the higher education in western Orissa is in a state of disarray. Many posts of teachers in the Higher Education Dept are lying vacant in the district, which is being represented by the Minister of State for Higher Education Bimbadhara Kuanr. Since the govt. is not recruiting teachers pleading financial crisis, the locals have demanded to prepare a special cadre list for the western part of the state and fill up the posts lying vacant by appointing teachers on ad hoc basis...Teachers are not showing interest to be posted in the colleges located at the western part of the state. Whoever is getting appointment in these colleges; they are trying for their transfer to the colleges at the coastal pockets. Hence most of the teachers' posts in these areas are lying vacant. As a result of which most of the time colleges in these areas remain closed, thereby, depriving the students of getting proper higher

education. This has become a usual problem of the western Orissa." (September 1 2002)[52]

The Koshali people really do not understand why their own state people located in the Costal Orissa have opposed the proposal for making Sambalpur University a central university when this only institution is serving the whole of the Koshala region whereas the Coastal Orissa cornered a total of seven universities. The power politics at state capital favour Utkal University to be made central university as a result of which the proposal to have a central university in Orissa has been lying in official document since long time. These un-helpful attitudes of the state government and Coastal people made Koshali people more aware that educational development of Koshala is not possible under the present Orissa state.

It was realized that when the whole of India is faster liberalizing under a globalizing world economy, if Koshala's half of the population cannot even read and write it may not be exaggerated to say that the region is really in the danger of marginalization. In an open economy increasingly driven by new technologies it is the formation of skills and knowledge that are crucial factors for a region to benefit from globalization. The feeling of the Koshali people that Orissa government has played a discriminatory role in addressing the basic human want to be knowledgeable in the case

[52] Dharitri (2002) 'Higher education in western Orissa in a state of disarray', September 1.

of Koshala relative to Coastal has been a crucial factor in their demand for a separate state.

VI
Deprivation in Access to Health Services

Over the years the Koshala region has emerged not only as the most poorest and illiterate region in Orissa but also the most deprived region in terms of health services. In an underdeveloped region like Koshala where majority of people stays below the poverty line the public healthcare institutions play crucial role in people's lives by providing access to preventive services, such as immunization, maternal healthcare and family planning services. However, it is most unfortunate that the people in Koshala region lacked the most basic health facilities which the people in Coastal region are getting, the Orissa government continues to expand relatively more public health services in Coastal region.

The essay summarizes the availability of primary health center (PHC) in Orissa suggests that the number of PHCs in Koshala and Coastal region were nearly balanced to start with, 90 in the Coastal region and 93 in the Koshala region. But by 2002 the state government has added about 699 PHCs in the Coastal region compared with mere 467 PHCs in the Koshala region. Considering the population coverage per PHC and per doctor one may likely to conclude that this addition is justified as the Coastal region has got a higher figure than Koshala. However this conclusion is misleading as there are large-scale vacancies of sanctioned doctor posts in the Koshala region[53]. The vacancies figure, which is available only for four Koshali districts namely Koraput, Malkangiri, Nabarangpur and Rayagada is as high as 136 positions of doctors in different grades. It is further reported that there were 356 vacancies of staff nurses, laboratory technicians, compounders and other class IV paramedical staff in the health centres including district headquarters hospitals of these districts. It was also found that the doctors and paramedical staff hailing from the coastal region hardly prefer to stay in the Koshala region even for a fortnight at a stretch and whenever they are transferred to the region they go on extending their leave under one pretext or another (Orissa Development Report 2002, pp. 295). Even the National Human Rights Commission (NHRC) has noted

with concern that the number of mobile health units operating without doctors are increasing in the KBK districts[54]. Therefore, in the name of public health services the Koshala region has got hospitals from the government without doctors and infrastructures.

Note: Data on PHC is for 2002 and that on doctors is for 1999-2000.

The access to health facilities is also determined by the location of health centres nearer to the human settlement. On this parameter also Koshala seems to be the most deprived region. One PHC in Koshala region covered about an area of 165 square kilometers as compared to 81 square kilometers in the case of Coastal region . In Orissa around 42 percent of blocks (131 in number) do not had a health centre within a

[54] Orissa.net (2002) 'NHRC pulls up State Government for starvation deaths', November 22.

radius of 12 km. of human settlement in 1985 of which only 14 were from the coastal region and the rest others were from the backward highland districts of undivided Koraput, Kalahandi, Phulbani, Sambalpur and the present Gajapati district[55]. Thus the health facilities in the Koshala region are relatively less accessible to the people over space than Coastal region.

As far as tertiary health services are concerned the Koshala region has been systematically marginalized. It has only one medical institution which can offer some specialty health services namely Vir Surendra Sai medical college and hospital. This college, which caters to the needs of the Koshali districts of Orissa and a sizable population from Chhatisgarh has been continuously neglected by the state health department over the years[56]. This resulting in faster deprivation of the Koshali people from whatever limited higher health services they are having. The hospital is reported to have vacancies of about 60 per cent posts of professors and 40 per cent posts of doctors, ill-equipped and badly maintained operation theatre, and don't have an intensive care unit for critical care cases[57]. This has already caused widespread resentment among the Koshali people including the 800 junior doctors and students of the Veer Surendra Sai Medical College. The Koshali people got a real shock when the government of Orissa decided to set-up the All India Institute of Medical Sciences (AIIMS) in Bhubaneswar with utter disregards to the public opinion in Koshala. When there is a super-specialty medical hospital already in Bhubaneswar (Kalinga Hospital) and another in Cuttack hardly 25 kilometers away from Bhubaneswar and also numerous hospitals with modern facilities in the capital city there was no justification for setting up the AIIMS in Bhubaneswar[58]. As the health services in Vir Surendra Sai medical college and hospital is in shambles Koshali people are forced to go to Cuttack or Bhubanswar for better health facilities traveling nearly 500 kilometers. It is meaningless to expect that when majority of the Koshali people who have hardly any purchasing power to buy food will be able to

55 Rath (1997) quoted in Orissa Development Report 2002, pp. 296; Rath, N. (1997). 'Odisare Anchalika Asamatulata: Byadhi O' Tara Upachara', The Samaja, 8-12 July, 1997 (Published in five parts in Oriya).

[56] Orissa.net (1998) 'This time, the hospital is sick', July 27.

[57] NDTV (2004) 'Doctors protest dismal conditions', January 23.

[58] Orissa.net (2003) 'Centre to set up AIIMS in Bhubaneswar', May 05

make to the far away state capital for medical facilities[59]. Nowhere in the history of Modern Indian states, will one find such an example where a state deprived its 40 percent of population the spatial access to health services merely for the sake of keeping everything in one region. This fact has strengthened the belief of the Koshali people that Orissa government largely dominated by the Coastal leaders are ruthlessly insensitive to even the humanly issue like health and the natural solution for this discrimination is being sought in the formation of a new state.

VII
Disparity in Infrastructural Developments

The availability and quality of general infrastructures such as transportation facilities like road networks, railways, airports, and ports; communication networks such as postal, telephones, and other telecommunication services; financial services like banking; access to electricity and water, etc. play a crucial role in the economic progress of different regions. As the development of these infrastructure services require huge financial resources and involves long gestation period, the state play the role of initiator in their development. The rationality of government provisions of these services is quite strong in the case of underdeveloped regions of the state. However, in Orissa the government had relatively focused more in building best infrastructures in the developed parts of Coastal region ignoring the continuing poor infrastructures in Koshala region marked by poor market, road, rail and telecommunication network and limited provisions of basic amenities like electricity and water.

This Essay summarizes the length of road and railway network per 100 square kilometer of area for Koshala as well as Coastal region. It can be seen that the Koshala have got relatively low level of spatial coverage by roads as compared to the Coastal region. Road networks cover 164 kilometer of area in the Coastal region whereas it is 138 kilometer in the Koshala region, the shortfall in the coverage is amounting to be 26 kilometer. There are 11

Koshali districts, which lacked the average area coverage by road enjoyed by the coastal districts, of which Malkangiri, Rayagada, Kandhamal, and

[59] Informal circle news indicate that the Central government had initially proposed to set-up AIIMS in the underdeveloped Koshala region at Bolangir district but the Orissa government has opposed the decision. This has also contributed to the large-scale resentment among the Koshali people.

Koraput represent the most deprived district. Three Koshali districts such as Boudh, Malkangiri, and Rayagada are without national highway. Apart from the relatively low availability, roads in Koshala region are of poor quality as compared to Coastal region. The rural road networks comprising of gram panchayat road, village road, and forest road formed the major junk of road network in the Koshala region and are non-asphalt roads, inherently uneven, pit, rough and cracked roads. The lack of concern of the state government to improve the road conditions in Koshala region has been another factor contributed to the discontentment of the Koshali people. The Koshala Sangharsha Vahini which is leading the movement for separate state has listed this poor road infrastructure be one important reason for 'why Koshal?'[60].

[60] "Our roads and transportation has been the least priority of Orissa government while it is busy in constructing dazzling roads and bridges in the coastal region'. This is the eighth factor in the list of reasons advanced for the creation of separate Koshala state. See the un-dated pamphlet 'Dear Koshala-loving friends, mothers and sisters, why Koshala state?' of the Koshala Sangharsha Vahini.

Although the railway route per square kilometer of area differs marginally between Koshala and Coastal, many Koshali districts like Boudh, Deogarh, Kandhamal, Malkangiri, Nawarangpur do not have access to the railways. Further the state government has neglected the region in terms of air-networks. While the first airdrome in Orissa was established during British rule at Tushura of the Koshali district of Bolangir, the Koshali region has been written off the air-links in the state. The Tushura airport has never been revived except that it is being kept under the Airport Authority of India.

In terms of the access to post communication services, on a per capita basis the availability of post office per lakh population seems to be not differing between Coastal and Koshala region but the availability of post office per 1000 square kilometers of area tends to differ to a great extent. In the Koshala region only 34 post offices per 1000 square kilometers are available against 78 post offices in the case of Coastal region . Therefore, this low spatial spread of post office suggest that there are several hamlets in the tribal hinterland districts of the Koshala region which even now not have access to the common medium of communication channel like a post office. Considering another indicator of the communication infrastructure, the number of telephone lines per 100 persons, Koshala appears to have better accessibility than Coastal region. However, excluding the outliers, (un-divided) Sambalpur and Sundergarh districts, all other Koshali districts such as Anugul, Bolagir, Koraput, Phulbani, and Kalahandi have lower number of telephone lines than the all-Coastal level thus suggesting that majority of Koshali districts are still lagging behind the Coastal region .

Source: Based on Centre for Monitoring Indian Economy (2000) Profile of Districts, October.

Note: Koshala and Coastal district figures are simple averages of districts belongs to respective region. In the process of averaging Angul has been assigned the same figure as that of undivided district of Dhenkanal.

The regional disparity in the availability of banking facilities in Orissa has been equally conspicuous with the Koshala region lying far behind the Coastal region. While the number of banking branches in the Koshala region is 5.6 per lakh population and 8.7 per 1000 square kilometer of area it is 6.1 per lakh population and 21.5 per 1000 square kilometer of area in the Coastal region. Except Debgarh, Sambalpur and Sundergarh, all other Koshali districts have lower population coverage by the banking branches as compared to the Coastal level. In the case of banking branches per 1000 square kilometer of area invariably all of the Koshali districts fall below the Coastal

level at a wider gap possible. Not only in terms of the number of banking branches available that the Koshala region has remain backward region in Orissa but also in terms of credit allocation it has been systematically left out. The banking system has provided a per capita credit of Rs. 1255 to the developed parts of the Coastal region which is one and half times higher than the per capita credit given to the underdeveloped Koshala region (only Rs. 820) . Koshali districts like Malkangiri with Rs. 354, Nabarangapur with Rs. 398, Debagarh Rs. 421, and Sonepur with Rs. 419 represent the four most lowly per capita credit receiving districts.

The Koshala-Coastal differential is also noticeable in the case of the access to electricity. On an average, every 8 out of ten villages in the Coastal region are electrified whereas this is the case of about every 6 villages in the Koshala region . There are many Koshali districts where the number of electrified villages was not even 5 out of ten villages such as Rayagada, Malkangiri, Koraput, Kandhamal, and Debagarh. Considering the access to electricity at household level reveals that only 19 percent of Koshali household have access to electricity as compared to 27 percent of Coastal household .

Now coming to the irrigation facilities it was found that overall Orissa has very low irrigation facility amounting to be only about 28 percent of the gross cropped area (GCA) . Like previous indicators of infrastructure, the Coastal region has higher irrigation coverage of about 31 percent of GCA, nearly 5 percentage points higher than the 26 percent of the Koshala region. It is unfortunate that the Koshala region, which has been chronically drought-ravaged, the state government has not made any visible progress in improving the irrigation potential in the region. Due to low irrigation facilities Koshali farmers are losing their main source of living recurrently due to low and erratic rainfall.

VIII
Cultural Marginalization

In the emergence of the demand for separate state in Orissa, cultural factor has also played an important role. The state government has systematically discriminated towards Koshali language and literature. The Oriya Sahitya Samiti responsible for promoting Oriya language and literature has habitually favoured the Coastal dialect by various promotional schemes like providing cheap financing, publishing and instituting literary awards. The Samiti's bias against the Koshali language can be seen from the fact that not a single book written in Koshali dialect till date has been financed by it. The growth of the Koshali literature like Koshali Ramayana, Mahabharata, drama and story books has been completely left to the few dedicated Koshali literaturist who without any support from the state government published these books with local publishers. Except the Sambalpur branch of the All India Radio Station (AIR), which provides programs in the Koshali language covering Koshali poem recitation, state support has been marginal in the promotion of Koshali language and literature. While Koshali people accepted the

Coastal dialect as a medium of study and even came forth in contributing to the literature based on it (e.g. Gangadhar Meher), it is not understandable for them that the Coastal people have actively discriminated the Koshali language. In the history of modern Orissa one will not find a single piece of evidence where the Coastal people have contributed anything to the cause of the Koshali language. Contrary to the promotion, most of the video album-making companies like Samrat and Siddharta based in the Coastal region are loose large to bring out Sambalpuri video cassates which are devastatingly filthy and distorted by copying Hindi songs and mixing them with Sambalpuri which undermines Sambalpuri as an independent language. The state, which is proud of its own diversity in language and literature and should have promoted Sambalpuri as an indispensable part of Oriya language, but evidently the State, has completely failed in doing so.

Likewise in the promotion of the Koshali arts and artists, the State support has been minimal. In the case of dance, while Orissa government is continuously promoting Odissi dance in Orissa as well as outside the state, the Koshali dance received the least focus of the government. This state-led discrimination against Koshali language, literature, music, dance, and arts has made Koshali people realize that their very identity is under danger under the present Orissa State. The way-out from this is thus sought in a new Koshala state dedicated to the cause of Koshali culture and language.

IX

Apathy towards Koshali Tourism Sectors

The Koshala region has got tremendous tourism potential for various places having significance as diverse as historical, artistic, religious, wildlife, waterfall and natural beauty. Appendix Table-7 provides a list of Koshali tourist places. The Koshala region occupied an important place in Indian religious history being a place of religious confluence of faiths like Saivism, Buddhism, Jainism, Vaisnavism, Tantrism and Sakti cult. All most all Koshali district are filled with some oldest and magnificent Shiva, Vishnu or Sakti temples drawing thousands of devotees from different parts of Orissa signifying that the region has been a great religious center in the past. The Chinese traveler and Buddhist scholar Hiuen T'sang during his visit of Dakhin Koshala has mentioned about a flowering Buddhist University of Parimal Giri (po-lo-mo-lo-ki-li), which had its campus on the picturesque Gandhamardan hills. The very name of a

Koshali district, Boudh, has been gained after it was once a significant Buddhist centre in Orissa. The discovery of ruins of an old Jain monastery in the Kohsali district of Koraput suggests the significance of Koshala region for this faith.

The Koshala region with its numerous forts (Amathguda, Asurgarh, Junagarh, Talguda), palaces (Jogindra Villa Palace, Bolangir Palace, Jeypore Palace), and inscriptions and paintings (Vikramkhol, Yogimatha) etc. is very fascinating for historical point of view. Its enchanting hills, green forest, dams, waterfalls, wildlife sanctuary, tribal life and culture make it a source of eternal scenic beauty. Many of the tourist places are of national and international significance. For instance, Hirakud standing across the great river Mahanadi is the longest dam of the world.

The Koshala region with its scenic beauty, which deserves an important place in the world tourism, has hardly any place even within the Orissa tourism map. The Orissa government has been actively promoting tourism spot in the Coastal region such as Puri, Konark, Nandankanan, Chandipur, Chilika, Dhauli etc. For the last four decades the tourism sector of the Koshala region has been completely ignored by the Department of Tourism and Culture. The argument that the limited resources of the state government have not permitted it to extent its focus to the Koshali tourist places may be partially right. However when one takes into account the relatively developed infrastructure in the Coastal region and the historical significance of Puri, Konark etc. (even listed as part of world heritage by UNESCO), the underdeveloped Koshala should have been given relatively greater focus. It is unreasonable to say that the state government has not found time in bringing out a list of Koshali tourist places along with the Coastal tourist places to say to the world that Orissa has more apart from Puri and Konark to give to the tourist. It is most unfortunate that the discriminatory approach of the state government has not led Orissa to fully realize its tourism potential in the Koshala region. The state discrimination in the form of not marketing Koshali tourist places, poor infrastructural facilities like bad road conditions, lack of accommodation, catering and transportation facilities, absence of local planning, and lack of the government support facilities and incentives to encourage private investment in the Koshali tourism sector has been the obstacles in promoting Koshala tourism. As a result of state apathy the share of Koshala region in the total

tourist arrival in the state is very minimal at 7% of the total tourists inflow during 1991- 97[61].

When other states like Kerala is being able to market its backwaters as an important tourist place it is sorry to note that Orissa government has not been able to market its own places when it has been endowed with great variety of significance ranging from historical to scenic beauty. The lack of creative approach of the Orissa government can be seen from just considering that even after such a long period Orissa government has not even given the thought of marketing the Debrigarh along with its caves as a tourist place of national significance as this is the place from where Veer Surendra Sai the great Koshali freedom fighter had waged a long struggle against British Raj. While the states like Haryana could market their dry hill as tourist places, unfortunately with it's unmatched greenery, wildlife, tribal culture and handicrafts, the state of Orissa could not. It is just unwillingness on the part of the government to promote Koshala tourism sector is the single most important reason why Koshala region has not got its place in the national and international tourism map. Had the tourism sector been exploited properly in the Koshala region, this alone could have been a powerful weapon against chronic poverty in the region. The Koshali people clearly realized that their tourist places will not be provided with required infrastructure and marketing under the Coastal dominated state of Orissa and thus a new state of Koshala is thought to be the only solution to this problem.

X

Concluding Remarks

The demand for Koshala state has risen in Orissa mainly on the ground of underdevelopment and state-led discrimination against the region for decades. Most of the Coastal people disregard the demand for a separate state and consider it as political without appreciating the real issues behind the demand. The number of agitations for Koshala state has greatly increased recently marked by boycotting the state formation day (Utkal Divas), listing Koshali as their language in the Census survey, and bandhs (strikes), etc. The rising popular support for a Koshala state calls for urgent attention of the politicians, policy makers and the people of the coastal region to set the parameters of

[61] Source: http://orissagov.nic.in/tourism/western.htm

state policies right. Otherwise it will be very difficult to defend the unified Orissa state when the Koshala region is being systematically denied its share of development and kept in rising poverty, unemployment, poor health, and illiteracy. It should be realized that the forces of cultural and linguistic similarity, which was a tremendous force in the formation of state in India in the past, have already lost their significance. Now the issue of development has emerged as the most imperative criterion in the reorganization of states in India[62]. The Koshali people, who initiated the demand for a unified Orissa state in the past, have democratic right to demand for a separate state in the face of their continuous marginalization.

The present paper is an attempt to throw light on some of the issues behind the increasing discontentment of the Koshali population in the present Orissa regime. These are the factors that need immediate consideration by the State Government.

What are the solutions?

The most important challenge for Orissa government is to ensure that the public expenditure doesn't remain spatially inequitable. This requires removing discriminatory attitude in the Government policies by objectively creating a database on the pattern of regional distribution of public expenditure so as to monitor and ensure that the developmental function of the state remains regionally balanced.

When redefining the public function with respect to regional diversity it is important that the urgent developmental needs of the underdeveloped region are identified and appropriate solutions are provided. From the analysis of the present paper, the following issues can be taken for consideration by the Orissa government.

Improving Efficiency of Anti-Poverty Measures:

The most pressing problem that needs to be tackled by the Orissa government is to address the rising poverty in the Koshala region. Over the years the state has so many welfare measures for poor, which have definitely enriched the jargons in the poverty- related literature but have failed to benefit the poor. To improve the efficiency of such programmes it is essential to correct the present BPL list so that these benefit the actual

[62] Kumar, Pradeep (2000) 'Demand for New States: Cultural Identity Loses Ground to Urge for Development', Economic and Political Weekly, August 26-September 2, pp. 3078-3082.

poor. It is important to note that without creating employment opportunities even the BPL cards can not ensured that the poor gets benefit from subsidized rice or get advantage from other benefits as the poor have been found to mortgage their BPL cards to local money lenders due to lack of purchasing power. In this context it is required that the state government ensures that every BPL household must gets an EAS (Employment Assurance Scheme) card and achieve the objective of providing 100 mandays of employment to each card holder at the prescribed wage rate. The root cause of failures in the effective implementation of anti-poverty measures is rampant corruption at the administrative level, low level of participatory governance involving civil society, and unawareness of beneficiaries about the programmes. Ruthless action against corruption, information diffusion at local level, proper supervision and monitoring of the programmes are required by the state. As the majority of the state employees in the Koshala region are from the Coastal region and they take least interest in the development of the region, it is essential that the number of Koshali people in the state administration should be increased, at least by the half of the size of administration. To achieve this objective at least 40 percent of the posts in the Koshala region, at all levels of administration from teachers to block development officers, should be reserved for the Koshali people. This is most crucial to make bureaucracy sensitive to the plight of the poor in the Koshala region.

Addressing the problems faced by migrant workers:

The Orissa government needs to take immediate steps in identifying the migrant families in the Koshala region and evolves appropriate support measures for them. It may not be possible for the government to ensure that the Koshali migrants are not subjected to exploitation in other states because of informal and illegal mode of migration through inter-state labour contractors, but the government can take preventive measures that discourage distress migration. The government can also collect information about migrant labour families at the village level through the village level workers (VLWs) and extension officers and ensure that they get minimum days of wage employment and they are covered under the food, social and health security programmes being implemented at the panchayat level. Collection of information on migrant families may not be a difficult

task as the government has already put in place the management information system (MIS) for tracking starvation and malnutrition cases and action taken at every level of the administration from gram panchayat level to district level[63]. However, the provision of employment measures can only help to check the distress out-migration in the short-run. Addressing the causes of drought like large-scale deforestation by preserving and creating new forest and strengthening the irrigation facilities would guarantee that agriculture does not fail during the time of drought.

Upgrading the Public Educational Services:

The Orissa government should take immediate steps to fill the large-scale vacant posts exist at primary, secondary, and tertiary level of education. Other areas that need urgent attention are opening of new schools in the remote rural areas, constructing school building, improving library and laboratory facilities. In the name of providing primary education to the Koshala region the government's effort to institute 'sikshya karmi' system must be replaced by the proper trained teachers to ensure quality of education. The region is in dire need of additional universities. The government should also push the proposal for making Sambalpur University a central university. Utkal University being in the capital city and having relatively better infrastructure, it does not make sense in demanding for central university status especially when another university of the state catering about 40 percent of state population does not even have basic infrastructure. It has been observed that majority of the lecturers, teachers, doctors, and nurses in the Koshala region are from the Coastal region and they usually do not stay in the region, spending whole of their energy to get transferred to their own region. As a result, the post of teachers and doctors are completely filled in the Coastal region whereas the Koshala region has been left with educational institutions without teachers and hospital without doctors. The solution to this lies in dividing the administrative staff, teachers, doctors and other employees between the two regions as done in the case of Union Public Service Commission. The Koshala cadre of state employees should be barred from getting transferred to the coastal region and vice-versa. The state should also take steps to start research institutes for developmental studies, physics, mathematics, etc, in the Koshala

[63] Orissa.net (2003) 'Government evolves info system to check hunger deaths', January 27.

region which would definitely encourage research on problems of the Koshala region which research institutes based in the Coastal region tend to ignore.

Strengthening Public Health Facilities:

The pathetic condition of public health services in the Koshala region demands that the criteria of 'one health centre within a radius of 12 km. of habitations be fulfilled. The large-scale vacancies in the hospitals situated in the Koshala region should be filled as early as possible and law to banning inter-regional transfer should be passed. The government should be rigid in giving registration to new private hospitals in the developed parts of the state and provide incentives for starting private hospital in the deprived region. As the whole Koshala region depends upon the Burla Medical College, for specialty services, is now in a state of disarray, the branch of AIIMS should be shifted from Bhubaneswar to any one of the Koshala districts. To ensure that specialized doctors have easy access to the AIIMS, the airdrome at Tusura should be revived. By shifting AIIMS, the Coastal population will not loose anything as there are already super specialty hospital in Bhubaneswar and Cuttack. This would not only reduce the patient pressures from the Koshala region in the Coastal hospitals but also earn the good will of the brothers and sisters of Koshala region. The infrastructure facility in other hospitals of the Koshala region is highly inadequate requires immediate attention by the government.

Improving Infrastructure Availability:

Building and improving the quality of roads, railways, postal, telecommunication, banking, irrigation and power related infrastructure is a high priority for the Koshala region simply because the region has remained worse for years together. Without improving such basic facilities Orissa cannot be expected to reap gains from exploiting minerals, water, and forest resources of the Koshala region and also the state cannot attract the private investment including foreign investment flows as they are strongly and positively related with availability of infrastructure. Upgrading different kinds of infrastructure will not only help Orissa build new productive capacity in the resource-rich Koshala region but also ensure that the whole of the state benefit from increase in employment, efficiency and income.

Promoting Koshali language, Literature and Culture:

The Orissa government needs to undertake special efforts to preserve and promote the language, literature and culture of its half of the population living in the Koshala region. The overall cultural heritage of the state will greatly enrich by promoting the Koshali culture namely dances, drama, literature, ethnic food, clothing, and festivals. Inclusion of Koshali books for consideration of Oriya Sahitya Academy, promoting Koshali dance as per Oddissi, establishment of research institutes for improving Koshali heritage, providing incentives for new books in Koshali language, promoting Koshali saree (Sambalpuri saree), etc. will definitely strengthen the cultural diversity of the Orissa and can minimize the feeling of marginalization of the Koshali people. Further it should not be forgotten that the original homeland of the religious icon of the Coastal region, Lord

Jagannath, was the Koshala region from where he was brought to Puri[64]. An inclusive approach to the cultural diversity can alone ensure that the present Orissa state remain as one, strong and developed.

Developing Koshali Tourism Sectors:

By focusing only on Puri, Konark and few other tourist spots within the Coastal region, Orissa missed the opportunities to reap the benefit from tremendous tourism potential that it possess in terms of historical, religious, tribal and scenic significance. The enchanting meadows, singing streams, dams, wildlife, caves, temples, palaces, and forts of Koshala region could tremendously contribute Orissa in getting a unique place in the world tourism. An integrated tourism package covering sea-beaches of the Coastal region to the beautiful hills of the Koshala region can ensure the elevation of Orissa to the top-most attractive place for tourists in India. The government efforts in establishing a separate Koshala Tourism Promotion Section in the department of tourism and culture, information provision and marketing of Koshali tourist places, upgrading tourist infrastructures, creating human resource skills required for tourism, and improving the general conditions of roads are some of the instruments that can be considered for the promotion of the Koshala tourism sector.

[64] Pragativadi (2003) 'Retired Prof puts Western Orissa as the original homeland of Lord Jagannath', Editorial, December 04.

While undoing the underdevelopment of the Koshala region lies in addressing the above issues, the degree of government efforts and success form the bottom line that can contain or explode the popular demand for a new state in Orissa. Whether the Koshali people with their fifty years of accumulated backlog of hunger, poverty, illiteracy, and malnutrition would provide another chance to the Orissa government to correct its past policies of developmental exclusions remains to be seen. For a large country like India the movements for smaller states like Koshala, Telengana, and Vidarbha provides an opportunity for strengthening decentralization process as well as for ensuring that development percolates to the neglected regions. In this context, if the democratic movement for a Koshala state in Orissa settled for a new state it should be heartily welcomed. However, it is the time that can tell us who wins at the end - whether the urge for development or saga of underdevelopment?

REFERENCE

Arjan de Haan, A. and A. Dubey (2003) 'Extreme deprivation in remote areas in India: social exclusion as explanatory concept', paper presented at Manchester conference on Chronic Poverty, April 2003.

Asia Times (1999) 'Hunger, disease stalked Orissa long before cyclone', November 17. Chowdhury, A. R. (2004) 'In search of India Shining', *Hindu Business Line*, April 19. Daily Excelsior (2003) 'Demand for Koshala state gains momentum in Orissa', June 01. Deccan Herald (2004) 'Cry for Koshala', January 04.

Dharitri (2002) 'Higher education in western Orissa in a state of disarray', September 1. Dreze, J. (2001) 'More Lifelines', *Times of India*, September 17.

Frontline (2001) 'Ferment in Orissa: Even as the movement seeking statehood for western Orissa gains momentum, the State government renews its demand for special category status for Orissa', Vol.18, Issue 15, Jul. 21 - Aug. 03.

Government of Orissa (1991) *Statistical Abstract of Orissa 1991*, Directorate of Economics and Statistics, Bhubaneswer.

Government of Orissa (1996) *Education In Orissa 1995-96*, Directorate of Elementary Education (Statistical Cell), Bhubaneswer.

Government of Orissa (2002) Orissa Development Report 2002, Planning Commission and Government of Orissa, Nabakrushna Choudhury Centre for Development Studies. Available at http://planningcomission.nic.in/plans/stateplan/stplsf.htm

Government of Orissa (2003) *Orissa Economic Survey 2002-2003*, Bhubaneswar. Hindu (2001) 'Orissa deaths: Abject poverty comes into focus', August 31.

Hindu (2003) 'Stir for 'Koshala State' to be intensified', October 20. Hindu (2004) 'Searching for jobs, they leave their votes behind', April 03.

Hindustan Times (2003) 'Demand for separate Koshala state gets boost in western Orissa' November 17.

Hindustan Times (2003) 'MLA seeks statehood for western Orissa', October 14. Hindustan Times (2004) '32 lakh students dropping out of Orissa schools every year',

February 4.

Hindusthan Times (2003) 'Starving mother sells baby for Rs. 10', December 19.

Indiainfo.com (2000) 'A new state out of Orissa in 5 years?', available at http://newsarchives.indiainfo.com/2000/10/06/kosala6.html

Indian Express (1998) 'Forced to choose: Stomach or slate', November 16.

Indian Express (2000) 'Drought spells disaster for the little women of Orissa', December 8.

Indian Express (2001) 'Danger -- drought ahead', February 17.

InterPress Service (1999) 'India: Loss of Forest Control Impoverishes Orissa Villagers', November 23.

Koshala Koshala Sangharsha Vahini (undated) 'Dear Koshala-loving friends, mothers and sisters, why Koshala state?', Central Office, Prabhuvakti Ashram, Godbhaga, Sambalpur.

Kumar, Pradeep (2000) 'Demand for New States: Cultural Identity Loses Ground to Urge for Development', Economic and Political Weekly, August 26-September 2, pp. 3078-3082.

Narasimham (2004) 'Money talks...and walks', *Humanscape*, Vol. XI, Issue III, March. NDTV (2001) 'Misuse of funds discovered in Orissa's Food for Work scheme', June 12. NDTV (2004) 'Doctors protest dismal conditions', January 23.

Orissa.net (1998) 'Child labour sold in Mumbai for four thousand rupees from Kondhamal district', October 16.

Orissa.net (1998) 'Starvation deaths alleged in Balangir dist HC seeks Govt report in 15 days', November 21.

Orissa.net (1998) 'This time, the hospital is sick', July 27.

Orissa.net (2000) 'Govt grilled over continuing hunger deaths', December 15. Orissa.net (2000) 'Hunger deaths trigger angry protests', December 08;

Orissa.net (2000) 'Sambalpur Municipality adopts resolution for Koshala state', February 11.

Orissa.net (2001) 'It's official – 95 pc live below poverty line', September 28. Orissa.net (2001) 'Thanks to Govt , they happily stay below poverty line', January 25. Orissa.net (2002) 'Anti-poverty schemes a farce in Orissa', December 10.

Orissa.net (2002) 'NHRC pulls up State Government for starvation deaths', November 22.

Orissa.net (2003) 'Centre to set up AIIMS in Bhubaneswar', May 05

Orissa.net (2003) 'Government evolves info system to check hunger deaths', January 27. Pragativadi (2003) 'Pro-Koshala campaigners gear up to intensify stir', December 13.

Pragativadi (2003) 'Retired Prof puts Western Orissa as the original homeland of Lord Jagannath', Editorial, December 04.

Rath, N. (1997). 'Odisare Anchalika Asamatulata: Byadhi O' Tara Upachara', The Samaja, 8-12 July, 1997 (Published in five parts in Oriya).

Sahu, N. K., P. K. Mishra and J. K. Sahu (2001) *History of Orissa*, Nalanda, Binod Behari: Cuttack.

Samaj (2001) 'Health System in Total Disarray in the Tribal Region of Orissa', August 07.

Sinha, B. N. (1999) *Geography of Orissa*, National Book Trust: New Delhi

Times of India (2001) 'Centre withholds Rs 130 cr aid for Kashipur', September 05; Times of India (2001) 'In Orissa, funds for the poor are siphoned by babus', September

01.

Times of India (2001) 'Orissa govt takes action against three officials', September 04. Times of India (2002) 'Even the royals are now poor in Orissa', January 07.

Times of India (2003) '18 years later: The poverty show goes on', June 18.

Times of India (2003) 'Three Dalit minors rescued from rape, bondage', August 28. Utkal Sambad (2004) 'Improper Utilization of funds in KBK districts: Planning

Commission expresses concern', March 4.

Utkal Sambad (2004) 'Starvation deaths, child selling incidents under Naveen govt. on rise', March 4.

Yahoo.com (2004) 'Migrant labourers in drought-hit Orissa to boycott polls', March 24, available at http://in.news.yahoo.com/040324/139/2c6ou.html.